Cross Stitch

Oh, Baby!

2

8

14

20

Stitch these charming designs for the little one in your life!

26   **28**   **30**

LEISURE ARTS, INC. • Maumelle, Arkansas

Designed by Gail Bussi

The 1871 children's poem by Englishman Edward Lear comes to life in this sweet design. It's the perfect whimsical addition to a little one's bedroom.

The Owl and the Pussycat

Note: Please read all instructions on page 32 before beginning.

Stitch Count = 125w × 99h

FABRIC SIZE

- One 17" × 15" (43.2cm × 38.1cm) piece of 28-ct. Summer Sky Hand-Dyed Jobelan® by Wichelt Imports (stitched over two threads)

DESIGN SIZE

- 25-ct. = 10" × 7⅞" (25.4cm × 20.0cm)
- 28-ct. = 8⅞" × 7" (22.5cm × 17.8cm)
- 32-ct. = 7⅞" × 6⅛" (20.0cm × 15.6cm)

INSTRUCTIONS

Center the design and begin stitching over two fabric threads. Work cross stitches, half cross stitches, and quarter stitches with two strands of cotton embroidery floss. To maximize color changes of DMC® Color Variations floss, complete each cross stitch before moving on to the next one. Use one strand of cotton embroidery floss to work backstitches and French knots. Use a pressing cloth to carefully iron the needlework from the back before framing as desired.

CROSS STITCH

ANCHOR		DMC	COLOR
399	L	318	Light Steel Gray
168	R	597	Turquoise
167	A	598	Light Turquoise
303	T	742	Light Tangerine
301	P	744	Pale Yellow
300	Y	745	Light Pale Yellow
1012	J	754	Light Peach
390	E	822	Light Beige Gray
244	C	987	Dark Forest Green
242	D	989	Forest Green
903	N	3032	Medium Mocha Brown
1048	K	3776	Light Mahogany
899	G	3782	Light Mocha Brown
273	U	3787	Dark Brown Gray
311	V	3827	Pale Golden Brown
029	B	3831	Dark Raspberry
026	H	3833	Light Raspberry
002	·	3865	Winter White

DMC COLOR VARIATIONS		COLOR
4100	Z	Summer Breeze

FRENCH KNOT

ANCHOR		DMC	COLOR
273	●	3787	Dark Brown Gray

BACKSTITCH

ANCHOR		DMC	COLOR
168	——	597	Turquoise
244	——	987	Dark Forest Green
273	——	3787	Dark Brown Gray
779	——	3809	Very Dark Turquoise
029	——	3831	Dark Raspberry

▢ Bright blue area indicates last row of previous section of design.

Project Tip

Stitching with Over-Dyed Floss

In areas stitched with DMC® Color Variations floss, complete each cross stitch in full before moving on to the next one. This method will keep the gradual color changes of the floss in your stitching. The traditional method of completing an entire row of half cross stitches before going back and finishing the full cross stitches will result in a more uniform color because the subtle variations will be lost.

The Owl and the Pussycat B

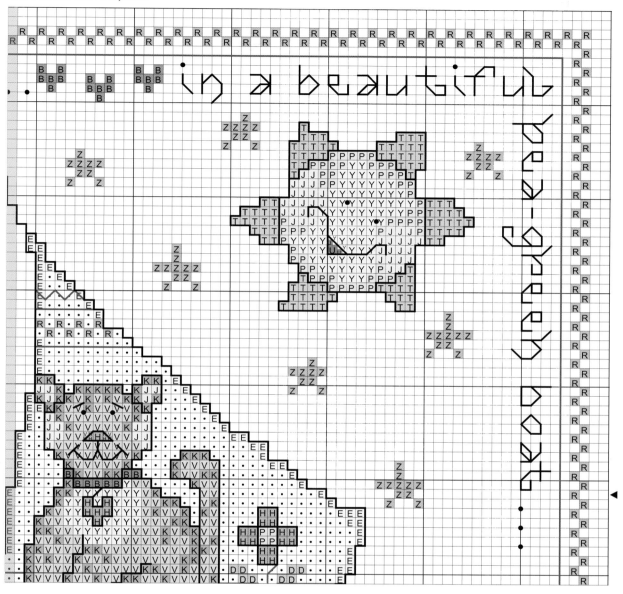

CROSS STITCH

ANCHOR		DMC	COLOR
399	L	318	Light Steel Gray
168	R	597	Turquoise
167	A	598	Light Turquoise
303	T	742	Light Tangerine
301	P	744	Pale Yellow
300	Y	745	Light Pale Yellow
1012	J	754	Light Peach
390	E	822	Light Beige Gray
244	C	987	Dark Forest Green
242	D	989	Forest Green
903	N	3032	Medium Mocha Brown

CROSS STITCH

ANCHOR		DMC	COLOR
1048	K	3776	Light Mahogany
899	G	3782	Light Mocha Brown
273	U	3787	Dark Brown Gray
311	V	3827	Pale Golden Brown
029	B	3831	Dark Raspberry
026	H	3833	Light Raspberry
002	•	3865	Winter White

DMC COLOR VARIATIONS			COLOR
4100	Z		Summer Breeze

FRENCH KNOT

ANCHOR	DMC	COLOR
273	•	3787	Dark Brown Gray

BACKSTITCH

ANCHOR	DMC	COLOR
168	597	Turquoise
244	987	Dark Forest Green
273	3787	Dark Brown Gray
779	3809	Very Dark Turquoise
029	3831	Dark Raspberry

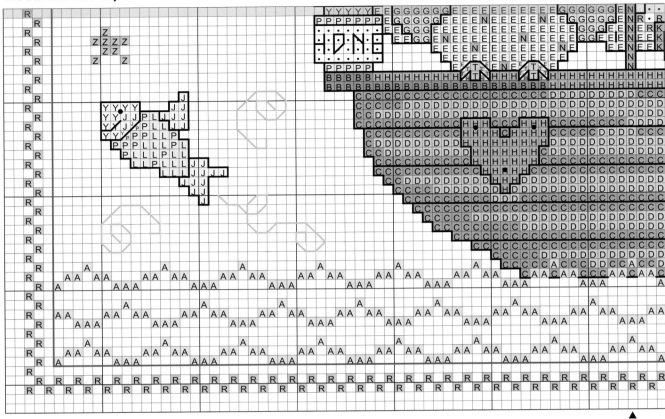

Project Tip

Go With the Grain

Embroidery floss comes in a twisted length made up of six strands that must be separated before stitching can begin. Even though the floss looks perfectly uniform, it does have a grain. By following the grain you lessen the wear and tear on your thread as you draw it through the fabric. This results in stitches that look smoother and silkier. To find the grain direction, cut a length of floss. Loop the thread over so both the cut ends lie next to each other. Do not allow the two ends to bundle together as you must be able to differentiate between them. Holding the cut lengths close together, about ½" from the tips, use one finger of your free hand to gently tap the cut ends. Watch carefully—the end that balloons most is the end that should be threaded through your needle (and is the shorter tail). This tiny extra step can make a significant difference to the look of your finished stitching!

The Owl and the Pussycat D

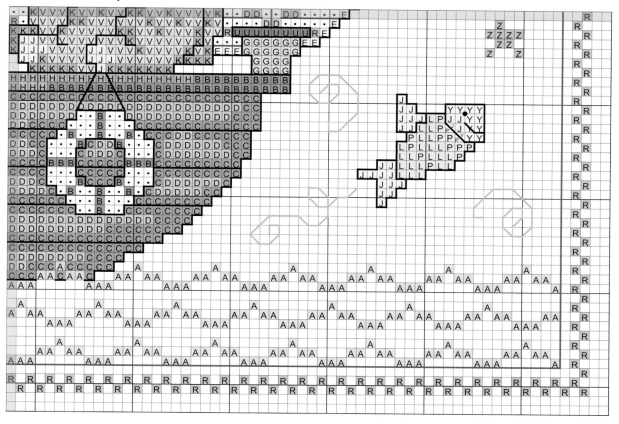

CROSS STITCH

ANCHOR		DMC	COLOR
399	L	318	Light Steel Gray
168	R	597	Turquoise
167	A	598	Light Turquoise
303	T	742	Light Tangerine
301	P	744	Pale Yellow
300	Y	745	Light Pale Yellow
1012	J	754	Light Peach
390	E	822	Light Beige Gray
244	C	987	Dark Forest Green
242	D	989	Forest Green
903	N	3032	Medium Mocha Brown
1048	K	3776	Light Mahogany
899	G	3782	Light Mocha Brown
273	U	3787	Dark Brown Gray
311	V	3827	Pale Golden Brown
029	B	3831	Dark Raspberry
026	H	3833	Light Raspberry
002	·	3865	Winter White

DMC COLOR VARIATIONS			COLOR
4100	Z		Summer Breeze

FRENCH KNOT

ANCHOR		DMC	COLOR
273	●	3787	Dark Brown Gray

BACKSTITCH

ANCHOR		DMC	COLOR
168	——	597	Turquoise
244	——	987	Dark Forest Green
273	——	3787	Dark Brown Gray
779	——	3809	Very Dark Turquoise
029	——	3831	Dark Raspberry

Bright blue area indicates last row of previous section of design.

The Owl and the Pussycat Chart Diagram

A	B
C	**D**

Designed by Joan Elliott

Bath Time Fun

Make a baby's bath extra fun—and extra adorable—with this hooded towel, burp towel, and bath mitt! Turtles in swim caps and cute bunnies make the set as irresistible as a baby's smile. What a special gift for a new arrival!

STITCH COUNT
Hooded Baby Towel = 157w × 78h
Burp Towel = 94w × 33h
Bath Mitt = 63w × 31h

FABRIC SIZE
- One 30" × 34" (76.2cm × 86.4cm) White French Terry Cloth Hooded Baby Towel with 14-ct. aida cloth hood by Charles Craft
- One 12" × 18" (30.5cm × 45.7cm) White French Terry Cloth Burp Towel with 2½"-high 14-ct. aida cloth design area by Charles Craft
- One 5" × 8" (12.7cm × 20.3cm) White French Terry Cloth Bath Mitt with 2¼"-high 14-ct. aida cloth band by Charles Craft

HOODED BABY TOWEL DESIGN SIZE
- 14-ct. = 11¼" × 5⅝" (28.6cm × 14.3cm)

BURP TOWEL DESIGN SIZE
- 14-ct. = 6¾" × 2⅜" (17.1cm × 6.0cm)

BATH MITT DESIGN SIZE
- 14-ct. = 4½" × 2¼" (11.4cm × 5.7cm)

INSTRUCTIONS
For each piece, center the design on the aida cloth panel and begin stitching. Work cross stitches with two strands of cotton embroidery floss. Use one strand of cotton embroidery floss to work all backstitches, straight stitches, and French knots. Use the alphabet on page 13 to personalize the hooded towel, centering the name in the space on the bottom of the hooded towel design.

Note: Please read all instructions on page 32 before beginning.

CROSS STITCH

ANCHOR		DMC	COLOR
002	•	White	White
095	J	153	Very Light Violet
399	4	318	Light Steel Gray
977	E	334	Medium Baby Blue
398	V	415	Pearl Gray
096	N	554	Light Violet
168	K	597	Turquoise
167	W	598	Light Turquoise
303	T	742	Light Tangerine
302	G	743	Medium Yellow
301	A	744	Pale Yellow
257	U	905	Dark Parrot Green
256	Z	906	Medium Parrot Green
255	Y	907	Light Parrot Green
209	7	912	Light Emerald Green
204	M	913	Medium Nile Green
381	B	938	Ultra Dark Coffee Brown
075	P	962	Medium Dusty Rose
073	H	963	Ultra Very Light Dusty Rose
888	R	3045	Dark Yellow Beige
887	L	3046	Medium Yellow Beige
852	S	3047	Light Yellow Beige
025	D	3716	Very Light Dusty Rose
140	F	3755	Baby Blue
9159	C	3841	Pale Baby Blue

FRENCH KNOT

ANCHOR		DMC	COLOR
977	•	334	Medium Baby Blue
168	•	597	Turquoise
303	•	742	Light Tangerine
381	•	938	Ultra Dark Coffee Brown

BACKSTITCH

ANCHOR		DMC	COLOR
977	——	334	Medium Baby Blue
303	——	742	Light Tangerine
381	——	938	Ultra Dark Coffee Brown

STRAIGHT STITCH

ANCHOR		DMC	COLOR
381	——	938	Ultra Dark Coffee Brown

Note: For personalization, use alphabet on page 13.

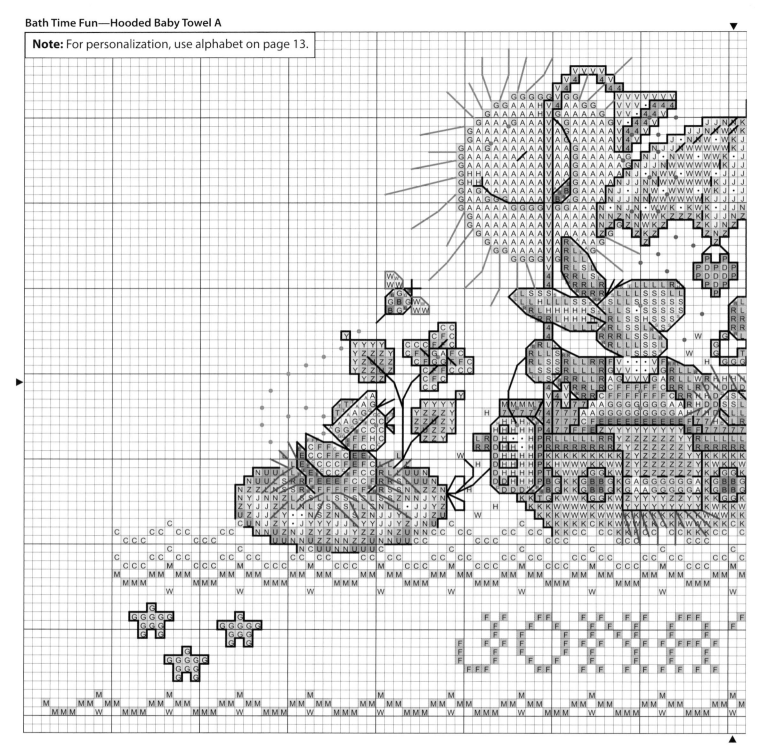

CROSS STITCH				CROSS STITCH				CROSS STITCH			
ANCHOR		DMC	COLOR	ANCHOR		DMC	COLOR	ANCHOR		DMC	COLOR
002	•	White	White	167	W	598	Light Turquoise	209	7	912	Light Emerald Green
095	J	153	Very Light Violet	303	T	742	Light Tangerine	204	M	913	Medium Nile Green
399	4	318	Light Steel Gray	302	G	743	Medium Yellow	381	B	938	Ultra Dark Coffee Brown
977	E	334	Medium Baby Blue	301	A	744	Pale Yellow	075	P	962	Medium Dusty Rose
398	V	415	Pearl Gray	257	U	905	Dark Parrot Green	073	H	963	Ultra Very Light Dusty Rose
096	N	554	Light Violet	256	Z	906	Medium Parrot Green	888	R	3045	Dark Yellow Beige
168	K	597	Turquoise	255	Y	907	Light Parrot Green	887	L	3046	Medium Yellow Beige

Bath Time Fun—Hooded Baby Towel B

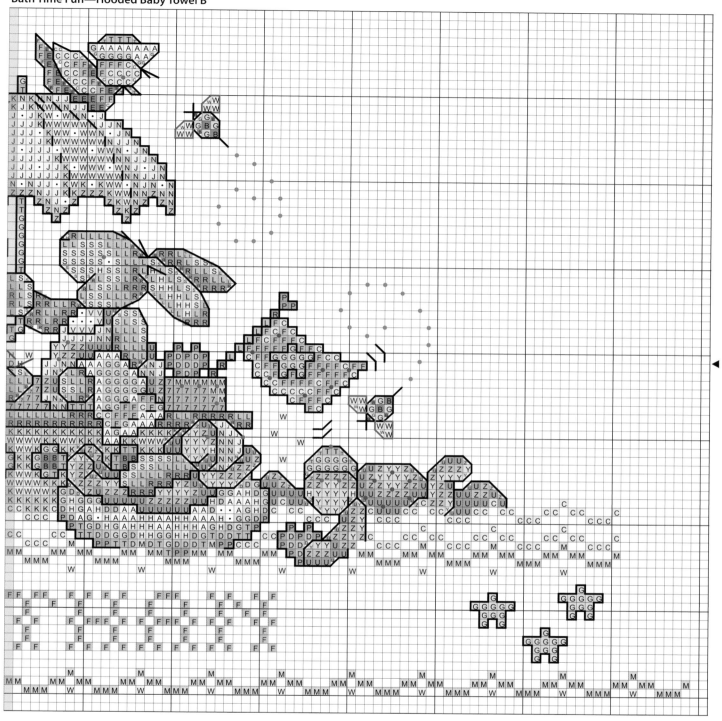

CROSS STITCH

ANCHOR		DMC	COLOR
852	S	3047	Light Yellow Beige
025	D	3716	Very Light Dusty Rose
140	F	3755	Baby Blue
9159	C	3841	Pale Baby Blue

FRENCH KNOT

ANCHOR		DMC	COLOR
977	•	334	Medium Baby Blue
168	•	597	Turquoise
303	•	742	Light Tangerine
381	•	938	Ultra Dark Coffee Brown

BACKSTITCH

ANCHOR		DMC	COLOR
977	——	334	Medium Baby Blue
303	——	742	Light Tangerine
381	——	938	Ultra Dark Coffee Brown

STRAIGHT STITCH

ANCHOR		DMC	COLOR
381	——	938	Ultra Dark Coffee Brown

**Bath Time Fun—
Hooded Baby Towel
Chart Diagram**

A	B

Bright blue area indicates last row of previous section of design.

Bath Time Fun—Burp Towel A

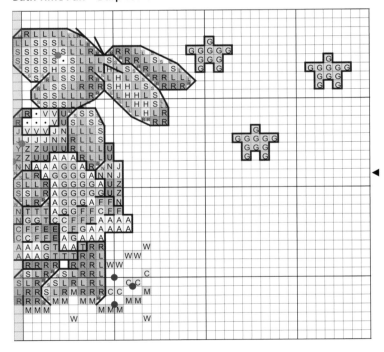

Bath Time Fun—Burp Towel B

CROSS STITCH

ANCHOR		DMC	COLOR
002	·	White	White
095	J	153	Very Light Violet
399	4	318	Light Steel Gray
977	E	334	Medium Baby Blue
398	V	415	Pearl Gray
096	N	554	Light Violet
168	K	597	Turquoise
167	W	598	Light Turquoise
303	T	742	Light Tangerine
302	G	743	Medium Yellow
301	A	744	Pale Yellow
257	U	905	Dark Parrot Green
256	Z	906	Medium Parrot Green
255	Y	907	Light Parrot Green
209	7	912	Light Emerald Green
204	M	913	Medium Nile Green
381	B	938	Ultra Dark Coffee Brown
075	P	962	Medium Dusty Rose
073	H	963	Ultra Very Light Dusty Rose
888	R	3045	Dark Yellow Beige
887	L	3046	Medium Yellow Beige
852	S	3047	Light Yellow Beige
025	D	3716	Very Light Dusty Rose
140	F	3755	Baby Blue
9159	C	3841	Pale Baby Blue

FRENCH KNOT

ANCHOR		DMC	COLOR
977	•	334	Medium Baby Blue
168	•	597	Turquoise
303	•	742	Light Tangerine
381	•	938	Ultra Dark Coffee Brown

BACKSTITCH

ANCHOR		DMC	COLOR
977	——	334	Medium Baby Blue
303	——	742	Light Tangerine
381	——	938	Ultra Dark Coffee Brown

STRAIGHT STITCH

ANCHOR		DMC	COLOR
381	——	938	Ultra Dark Coffee Brown

Bath Time Fun— Burp Towel Chart Diagram

Bath Time Fun—Bath Mitt

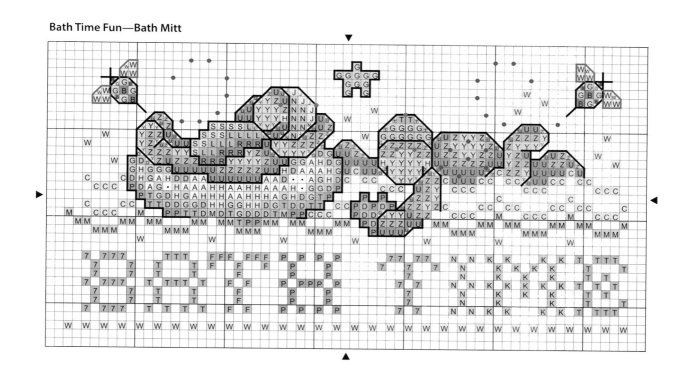

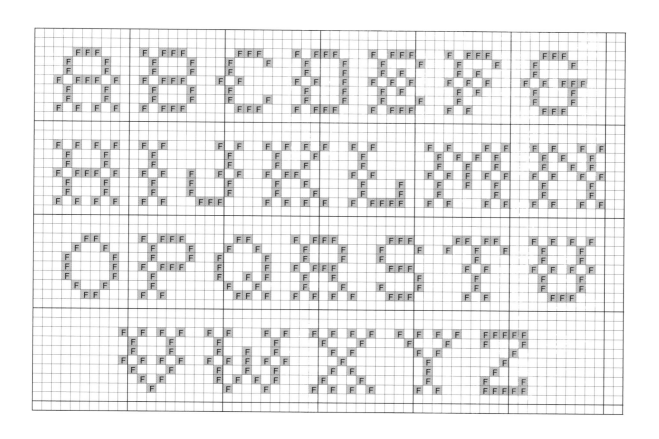

Designed by Gail Bussi

Featuring fluttering butterflies, buzzing bees, and budding flowers stitched in a pretty palette of pastels, this adorable piece is ideal for a little girl's room.

Note: Please read all instructions on page 32 before beginning.

Stitch Count = 131w × 131h

FABRIC SIZE
• One 17" × 17" (43.2cm × 43.2cm) piece of 28-ct. Antique White Jobelan® by Wichelt Imports (stitched over two threads)

DESIGN SIZE
• 28-ct. = 9⅜" × 9⅜" (23.8cm × 23.8cm)

FINISHING MATERIALS
• ½ yard of coordinating fabric for backing and binding
• One 12" × 12" piece of lightweight cotton batting
• One 12" × 12" piece of stiff interfacing
• Basting spray (optional)
• Matching sewing thread

GENERAL INSTRUCTIONS
Center the design and begin stitching over two fabric threads. Work cross stitches, half cross stitches, and quarter stitches with two strands of cotton embroidery floss. Work French knots and backstitches with one strand of cotton embroidery floss. Use a pressing cloth to carefully iron the needlework from the back before finishing.

FINISHING INSTRUCTIONS
Make sure the design is centered and trim the needlework to 12" × 12" (there should be approximately 1¼" border on each side of the stitched design). Cut a piece of backing fabric the same size. Place the back panel wrong side up on a work surface. Place the piece of cotton batting on top of it, then the piece of stiff interfacing, and then place the needlework piece right side up on top. (If desired, use basting spray between each layer.) Baste around the perimeter ¼" from the edge. Cut 3¾" strips of the coordinating fabric and piece together to form a strip at least 50" long. Fold in half along the length with wrong sides together and press to create a binding. With cut edges aligned and using a ⅝" seam allowance, sew the binding around the needlework side of the piece, folding to form a miter at each corner. Fold and press the binding to the back and hand-stitch in place. If desired, create a hanging loop by cutting a 2" × 13" strip from leftover fabric. Fold in half along the length with right sides together and press. Sew along the cut edge using a ¼" seam allowance, turn right sides out, and press. Attach ends to the top back of the wall hanging with a few hand stitches.

Butterfly Dreams A

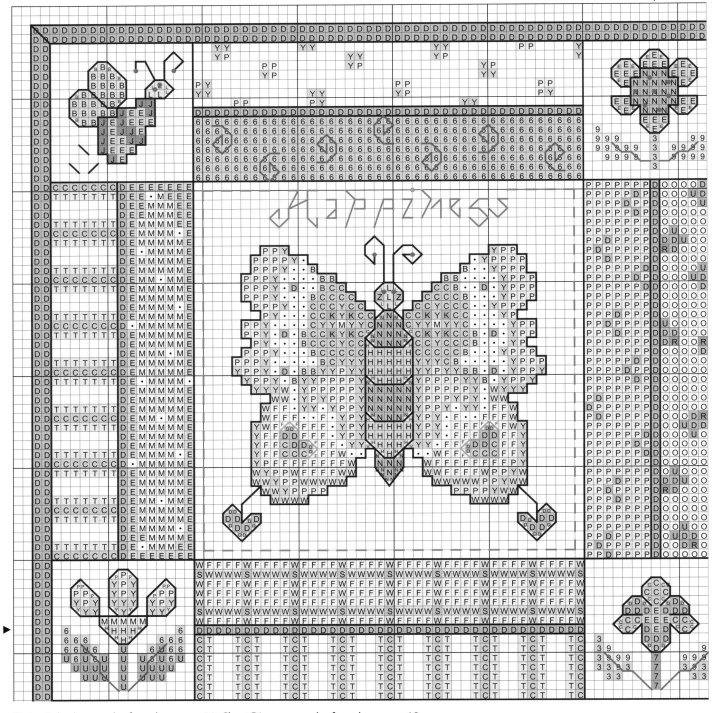

Note: Color key can be found on page 19. Chart Diagram can be found on page 18.

Butterfly Dreams B

Sewing Not Your Thing?
Talk to your local needlework store about recommending a finishing service. A good finisher can either complete the wall hanging as we've shown here or suggest one of the many other ways your piece could be finished.

Project Tip

97

Butterfly Dreams C

Project Tip

Keeping Fabric Clean in a Hoop

When using a hoop, try putting a sheet of white tissue paper in the hoop on top of the fabric. Tear away the tissue paper in the area where you are stitching. This keeps oils from your hands from getting on the fabric and helps keep the needlework piece free from stains. And whether you use a hoop or not, always wash and dry your hands completely before starting any stitching.

Butterfly Dreams Chart Diagram

A	B
C	D

Butterfly Dreams D

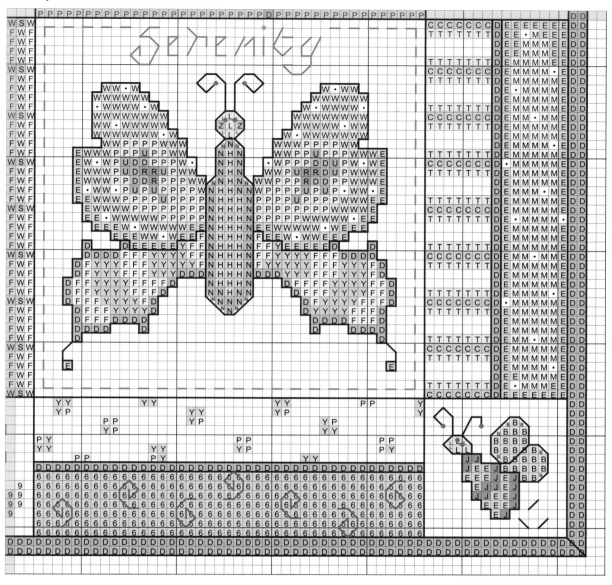

CROSS STITCH

ANCHOR		DMC	COLOR
002	·	White	White
095	P	153	Very Light Violet
109	K	209	Dark Lavender
215	3	320	Medium Pistachio Green
217	7	367	Dark Pistachio Green
214	9	368	Light Pistachio Green
1045	N	436	Tan
362	H	437	Light Tan
877	U	502	Blue Green
096	Y	554	Light Violet
301	E	744	Pale Yellow
300	M	745	Light Pale Yellow
234	B	762	Very Light Pearl Gray
271	T	819	Light Baby Pink
1011	L	948	Very Light Peach

CROSS STITCH

ANCHOR		DMC	COLOR
075	R	962	Medium Dusty Rose
073	C	963	Ultra Very Light Dusty Rose
903	V	3032	Medium Mocha Brown
129	W	3325	Light Baby Blue
025	D	3716	Very Light Dusty Rose
140	S	3755	Baby Blue
868	Z	3779	Ultra Very Light Terra Cotta
899	A	3782	Light Mocha Brown
393	J	3790	Ultra Dark Beige Gray
875	6	3813	Light Blue Green
386	O	3823	Ultra Pale Yellow
9159	F	3841	Pale Baby Blue

FRENCH KNOT

ANCHOR		DMC	COLOR
301	•	744	Pale Yellow
393	•	3790	Ultra Dark Beige Gray
029	•	3831	Dark Raspberry

BACKSTITCH

ANCHOR		DMC	COLOR
109	——	209	Dark Lavender
217	——	367	Dark Pistachio Green
877	——	502	Blue Green
075	——	962	Medium Dusty Rose
393	——	3790	Ultra Dark Beige Gray
029	——	3831	Dark Raspberry

Designed by Michele Johnson

There's no better gift for a mother-to-be than a handcrafted decoration for the nursery! This precious design is the ultimate in handmade: It's painted by two cute bunnies and stitched by you!

Note: Please read all instructions on page 32 before beginning.

Stitch Count = 173w × 115h

FABRIC SIZE
- One 20" × 16" (50.8cm × 40.6cm) piece of 14-ct. white aida

DESIGN SIZE
- 11-ct. = 15¾" × 10½" (40.0cm × 26.7cm)
- 14-ct. = 12⅜" × 8¼" (31.4cm × 21.0cm)
- 16-ct. = 10⅞" × 7⅛" (27.6cm × 18.1cm)

INSTRUCTIONS
Center the design and begin stitching. Work cross stitches and quarter stitches with two strands of cotton embroidery floss. Use one strand of cotton embroidery floss to work backstitches. Use a pressing cloth to carefully iron the needlework from the back before framing as desired.

CROSS STITCH

ANCHOR		DMC	COLOR
342	E	211	Lavender
977	L	334	Medium Baby Blue
310	S	434	Light Brown
1046	J	435	Very Light Brown
362	3	437	Light Tan
098	X	553	Violet
096	2	554	Light Violet
926	▽	712	Cream
305	V	725	Medium Light Topaz
361	7	738	Very Light Tan
387	U	739	Ultra Very Light Tan
301	<	744	Pale Yellow
300	Y	745	Light Pale Yellow
128	○	775	Very Light Baby Blue
187	∅	958	Dark Sea Green
186	?	959	Medium Sea Green

CROSS STITCH

ANCHOR		DMC	COLOR
073	#	963	Ultra Very Light Dusty Rose
185	∧	964	Light Sea Green
393	Z	3022	Medium Brown Gray
1040	4	3023	Light Brown Gray
397	☆	3024	Very Light Brown Gray
129	T	3325	Light Baby Blue
031	D	3708	Light Melon

BACKSTITCH

ANCHOR		DMC	COLOR
038	——	335	Rose
358	——	433	Medium Brown
178	——	791	Very Dark Cornflower Blue
162	——	825	Dark Blue
382	——	3371	Black Brown
236	——	3799	Very Dark Pewter Gray
188	——	3812	Very Dark Sea Green

Welcome Baby Bunnies A

Note: Color key can be found on page 21. Chart Diagram can be found on page 24.

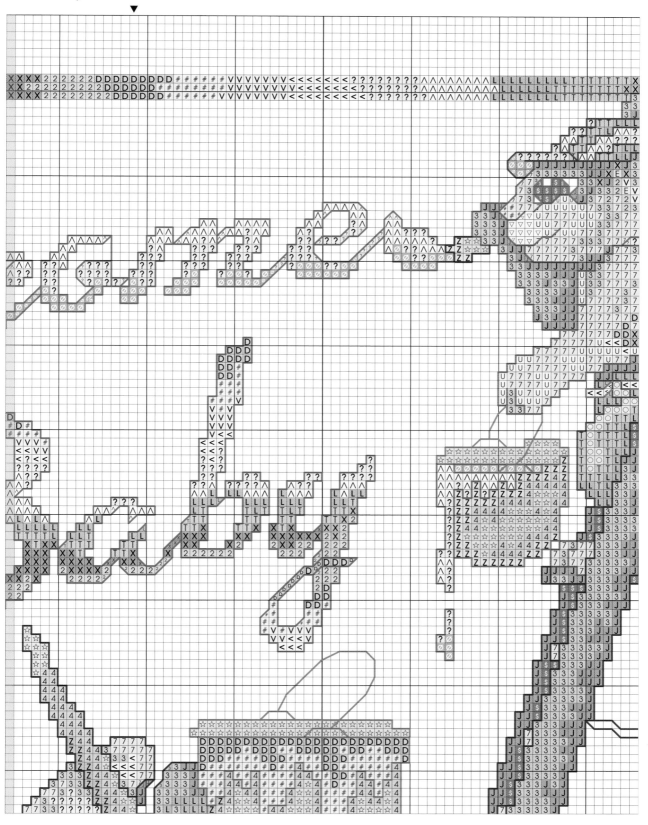

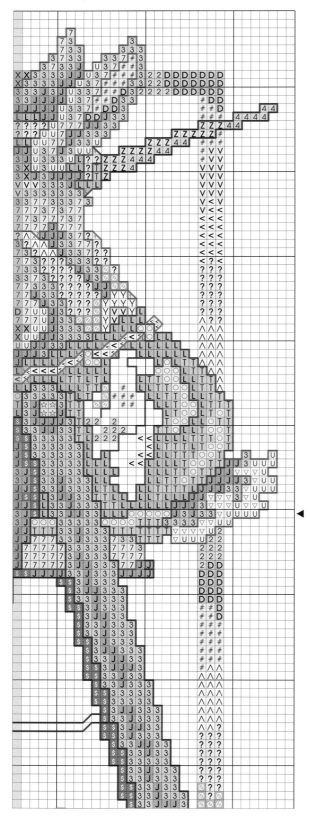

Welcome Baby Bunnies Chart Diagram

A	B	C
D	E	F

CROSS STITCH

ANCHOR		DMC	COLOR
342	E	211	Lavender
977	L	334	Medium Baby Blue
310	$	434	Light Brown
1046	J	435	Very Light Brown
362	3	437	Light Tan
098	X	553	Violet
096	2	554	Light Violet
926	▽	712	Cream
305	V	725	Medium Light Topaz
361	7	738	Very Light Tan
387	U	739	Ultra Very Light Tan
301	<	744	Pale Yellow
300	Y	745	Light Pale Yellow
128	○	775	Very Light Baby Blue
187	∅	958	Dark Sea Green
186	?	959	Medium Sea Green
073	#	963	Ultra Very Light Dusty Rose
185	∧	964	Light Sea Green
393	Z	3022	Medium Brown Gray
1040	4	3023	Light Brown Gray
397	☆	3024	Very Light Brown Gray
129	T	3325	Light Baby Blue
031	D	3708	Light Melon

BACKSTITCH

ANCHOR		DMC	COLOR
038	——	335	Rose
358	——	433	Medium Brown
178	——	791	Very Dark Cornflower Blue
162	——	825	Dark Blue
382	——	3371	Black Brown
236	——	3799	Very Dark Pewter Gray
188	——	3812	Very Dark Sea Green

▨ Bright blue area indicates last row of previous section of design.

Welcome Baby Bunnies D

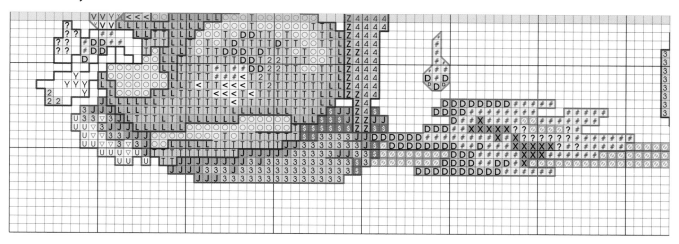

Welcome Baby Bunnies E

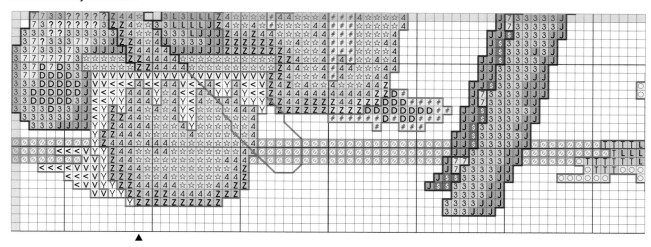

Welcome Baby Bunnies F

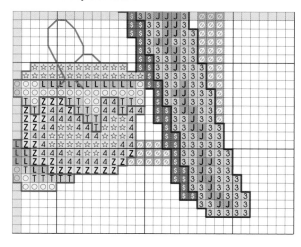

Project Tip

Working with Several Floss Colors
When working with frequent color changes, use several needles to avoid rethreading the same needle over and over. Work a few stitches in one color, bring the needle to the front of the fabric and put it aside. Introduce the next floss color and needle and continue.

Note: Color key can be found on page 24.

Designed by Michele Johnson

Little Lamb Sunshine

This fluffy friend—
who loves basking in the
sun—is the perfect addition
to a baby's room, whether you
stitch just this piece or pair it
with the other two lambs on
the following pages.

Note: Please read all instructions on page 32 before beginning.

Stitch Count = 84w × 84h

FABRIC SIZE
- One 14" × 14" (35.6cm × 35.6cm) piece of 14-ct. white aida

DESIGN SIZE
- 11-ct. = 7⅝" × 7⅝" (19.4cm × 19.4cm)
- 14-ct. = 6" × 6" (15.2cm × 15.2cm)
- 16-ct. = 5¼" × 5¼" (13.3cm × 13.3cm)

INSTRUCTIONS
Center the design and begin stitching. Work cross stitches with two strands of cotton embroidery floss. Use one strand of cotton embroidery floss to work backstitches. Use a pressing cloth to carefully iron the needlework from the back before framing as desired.

Note: Please read all instructions on page 32 before beginning.

Little Lamb Sunshine

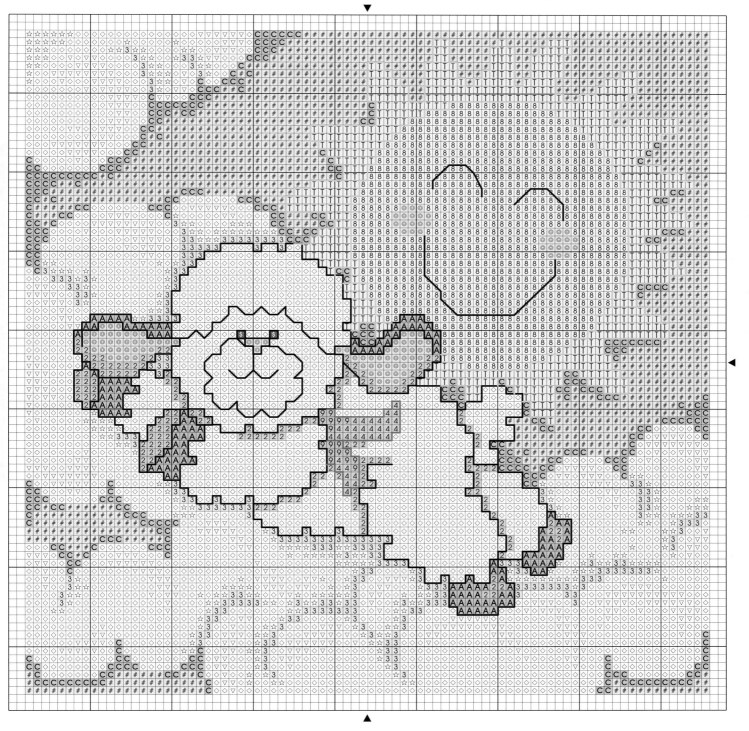

CROSS STITCH			
ANCHOR		DMC	COLOR
002	◇	White	White
403	$	310	Black
900	A	648	Light Beaver Gray
301	T	744	Pale Yellow
300	8	745	Light Pale Yellow
024	4	776	Medium Pink
161	C	813	Light Blue

CROSS STITCH			
ANCHOR		DMC	COLOR
023	◎	818	Baby Pink
160	#	827	Very Light Blue
9159	3	828	Ultra Very Light Blue
052	9	899	Medium Rose
847	2	3072	Very Light Beaver Gray
1037	☆	3756	Ultra Very Light Baby Blue
386	▽	3823	Ultra Pale Yellow

BACKSTITCH			
ANCHOR		DMC	COLOR
042	—	309	Dark Rose
403	—	310	Black
302	—	743	Medium Yellow

Designed by Michele Johnson

Little Lamb Raindrops

What child doesn't love playing in the rain? Your little one will adore this baby lamb frolicking among the raindrops and rainbow.

Note: Please read all instructions on page 32 before beginning.

Stitch Count = 84w × 84h

FABRIC SIZE
• One 14" × 14" (35.6cm × 35.6cm) piece of 14-ct. white aida

DESIGN SIZE
• 11-ct. = 7⅝" × 7⅝" (19.4cm × 19.4cm)
• 14-ct. = 6" × 6" (15.2cm × 15.2cm)
• 16-ct. = 5¼" × 5¼" (13.3cm × 13.3cm)

INSTRUCTIONS
Center the design and begin stitching. Work cross stitches with two strands of cotton embroidery floss. Use one strand of cotton embroidery floss to work backstitches. Use a pressing cloth to carefully iron the needlework from the back before framing as desired.

Little Lamb Raindrops

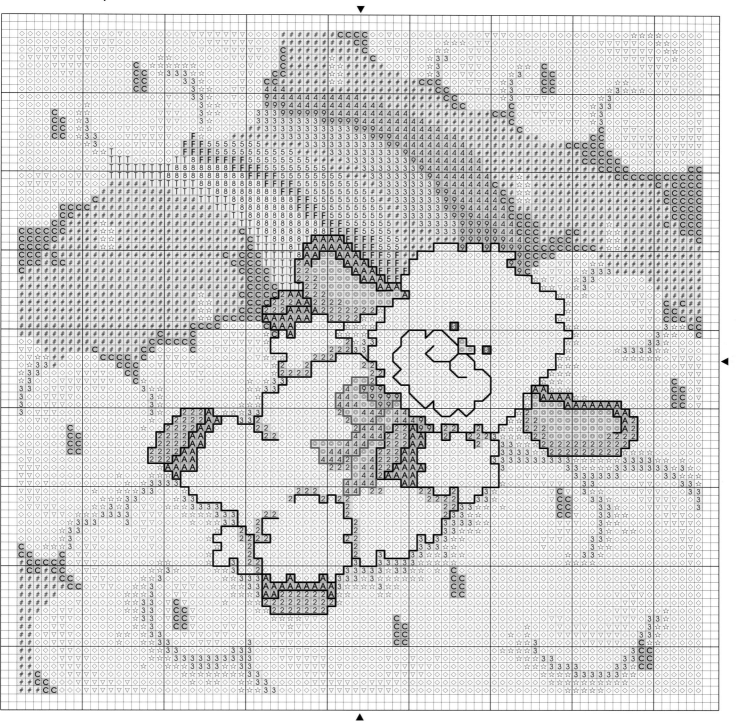

CROSS STITCH			
ANCHOR	DMC		COLOR
002	◇	White	White
403	S	310	Black
900	A	648	Light Beaver Gray
301	T	744	Pale Yellow
300	8	745	Light Pale Yellow
024	4	776	Medium Pink
161	C	813	Light Blue
023	◉	818	Baby Pink

CROSS STITCH			
ANCHOR	DMC		COLOR
160	#	827	Very Light Blue
9159	3	828	Ultra Very Light Blue
052	9	899	Medium Rose
203	F	954	Nile Green
206	5	955	Light Nile Green
847	2	3072	Very Light Beaver Gray
1037	☆	3756	Ultra Very Light Baby Blue
386	▽	3823	Ultra Pale Yellow

BACKSTITCH			
ANCHOR	DMC		COLOR
042	——	309	Dark Rose
403	——	310	Black

Little Lamb Good Night

This charming lamb will watch from above as your little one falls asleep.

Note: Please read all instructions on page 32 before beginning.

Stitch Count = 84w × 84h

FABRIC SIZE
- One 14" × 14" (35.6cm × 35.6cm) piece of 14-ct. white aida

DESIGN SIZE
- 11-ct. = 7⅝" × 7⅝" (19.4cm × 19.4cm)
- 14-ct. = 6" × 6" (15.2cm × 15.2cm)
- 16-ct. = 5¼" × 5¼" (13.3cm × 13.3cm)

INSTRUCTIONS
Center the design and begin stitching. Work cross stitches with two strands of cotton embroidery floss. Use one strand of cotton embroidery floss to work backstitches. Use a pressing cloth to carefully iron the needlework from the back before framing as desired.

Little Lamb Good Night

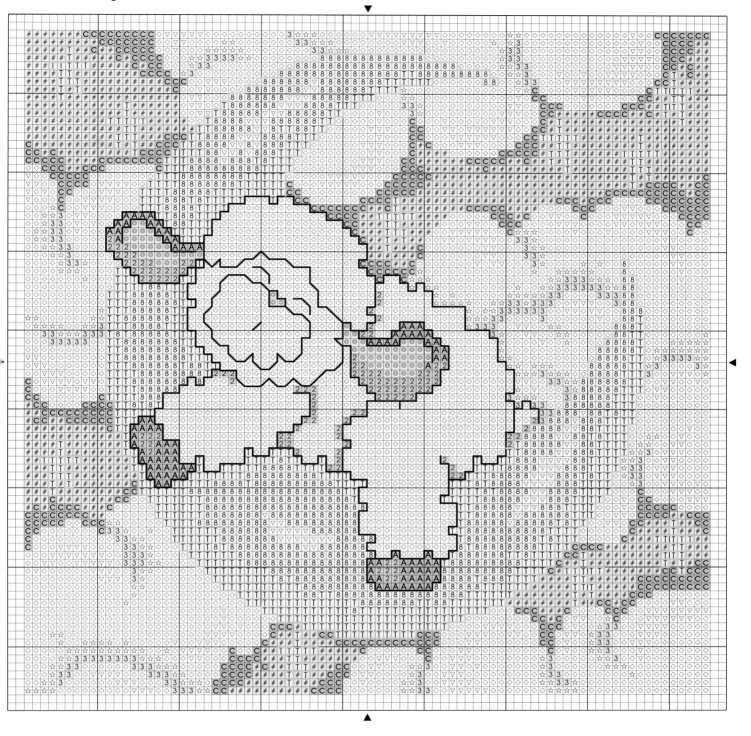

CROSS STITCH

ANCHOR		DMC	COLOR
002	◇	White	White
900	A	648	Light Beaver Gray
301	T	744	Pale Yellow
300	8	745	Light Pale Yellow
161	C	813	Light Blue

CROSS STITCH

ANCHOR		DMC	COLOR
023	◎	818	Baby Pink
160	#	827	Very Light Blue
9159	3	828	Ultra Very Light Blue
847	2	3072	Very Light Beaver Gray
1037	☆	3756	Ultra Very Light Baby Blue

CROSS STITCH

ANCHOR		DMC	COLOR
386	▽	3823	Ultra Pale Yellow

BACKSTITCH

ANCHOR		DMC	COLOR
403	▬	310	Black
302	▬	743	Medium Yellow

Getting Started

For most projects, the starting point is at the center. Every chart has arrows that indicate the horizontal and vertical centers. With your finger, trace along the grid to the point where the two centers meet. Compare a symbol at the center of the chart to the key and choose which floss color to stitch first. To find the center of the fabric, fold it into quarters and finger-crease.

Cut the floss into 15" lengths and separate all six strands. Recombine the appropriate number of strands and thread them into a blunt-tip needle. Unless otherwise indicated, use two strands of floss to work cross stitches, three-quarter cross stitches, half cross stitches, and quarter cross stitches, and use one strand of floss to work backstitches, straight stitches, and French knots.

To Secure Thread at the Beginning

The most common way to secure the beginning tail of the thread is to hold it on the wrong side of the fabric under the first four or five stitches.

To Secure Thread at the End

To finish, slip the threaded needle under previously stitched threads on the wrong side of the fabric for four or five stitches, weaving the thread back and forth a few times. Clip the thread.

Framing Your Pieces

Iron the finished needlework on the wrong side using a dry pressing cloth and medium temperature setting; do not steam. Accurately measure the length and width of your completed piece before purchasing a mat or frame. Consulting a professional framer or art supply store to mat and frame your design is recommended.

Cross Stitch

Make one cross stitch for each symbol on the chart. For horizontal rows, stitch the first diagonal of each stitch in the row. Work back across the row, completing each stitch. On most linen and evenweave fabrics, work the stitches over two threads as shown in the diagram. For aida cloth,

each stitch fills one square. You also can work cross stitches in the reverse direction. Remember to embroider the stitches uniformly—that is, always work the top half of each stitch in the same direction.

Quarter and Three-Quarter Cross Stitches

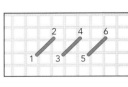

To obtain rounded shapes in a design, use quarter and three-quarter cross stitches. On linen and evenweave fabrics, a quarter stitch will extend from the corner to the center intersection of the threads. To make quarter cross stitches on aida cloth, estimate the center of the square. Three-quarter cross stitches combine a quarter cross stitch with a half cross stitch. Both stitches may slant in any direction.

Half Cross Stitch

A half cross stitch is a single diagonal or half a cross stitch. They are indicated on the chart by a diagonal colored symbol.

Backstitch

Bring the needle up from the back side of the fabric at odd numbers and go down at even numbers. Continue, keeping all the stitches the same length.

Straight Stitch

Bring the needle up from the back side of the fabric, then bring the needle down through the fabric in the desired spot to make a stitch of the desired length.

French Knot

Bring the threaded needle through the fabric and wrap the floss around the needle as shown. Tighten the twists and return the needle through the fabric in the same place. The floss will slide through the wrapped thread to make the knot.

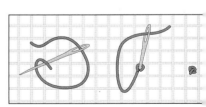

Produced by Herrschners, Inc., for distribution exclusively by Leisure Arts, Inc., 104 Champs Blvd., STE 100, Maumelle, AR 72113-6738, leisurearts.com.